MIDDLETON PLACE

A PHOENIX STILL RISING

Dedicated to the trustees, the staff and the volunteers of the Middleton Place Foundation.

And dedicated to descendants of the early Middletons of South Carolina who, with other generous benefactors of the Middleton Place Foundation, have given vitality, meaningfulness and sustainability to the historic preservation and interpretation of Middleton Place.

"MIDDLETON PLACE *offers a supreme example of how a great garden created two centuries ago has grown to mellow maturity… a garden in America as fine as any you could find in Europe.*"

MIDDLETON PLACE

A PHOENIX STILL RISING

By Charles Duell

with editorial and research assistance by

Barbara Doyle and Tracey Todd

Design by Lee Helmer

Middleton Place, still rising from its own ashes, epitomizes the high level of taste and culture, the grace and grandeur that were the hallmarks of 18th and 19th century South Carolina rice planting society. Internationally acclaimed for its distinctive historic and horticultural significance, the plantation spans two miles of waterfront that lie along the Ashley River approximately 20 miles upriver from Charleston. Here are North America's oldest and perhaps finest landscaped gardens; the Middleton Place House Museum with its collection of family portraits, silver and furniture; and the Plantation Stableyards with breeds of domesticated animals documented to have been in residence more than 150 years ago. Here also are craft shops and Eliza's House, a Reconstruction-era African American freedman's dwelling containing a permanent exhibit on slavery.

Two of America's Founding Fathers called Middleton Place home: Henry Middleton, a president of the First Continental Congress, and his son Arthur Middleton, a signer of the Declaration of Independence. Passing through female as well as male ownership, the land that became Middleton Place has been stewarded successively by members of the same family since the establishment of colonial Carolina in the late 1600s. It had been developed for agriculture and animal husbandry at least two generations before Henry Middleton began to lay out his gardens in 1741.

Middleton Place has survived the two American wars of secession, as well as several devastating hurricanes, a great earthquake and many economic challenges. Less than a century after the Revolution, it was ravaged in 1865 by conquering Union troops and two decades later by Charleston's Great Earthquake of 1886. By the close of the 19th century, Henry Middleton's magnificent gardens lay overgrown and neglected, his house and outbuildings in varying stages of decay. But the "bones" of the gardens endured, and the forlorn remains of the restored residential south flanker stood fast.

J. J. Pringle Smith

Heningham Lyons Ellett Smith

Then in 1916, Charlestonian J. J. Pringle Smith, a direct descendant of Henry Middleton, inherited his ancestors' showplace. He and his wife, the former Heningham Lyons Ellett of Virginia, moved to Middleton Place in 1925 and began the arduous work of returning it to its earlier glory. In 1941 the Garden Club of America presented the coveted Bulkley Medal to Middleton Place, and declared it to be not only the oldest but also, the most important and most interesting garden in America. The property, as it now stands, is a vibrant testimonial to the Smiths' pioneering devotion to restoration, conservation and historic preservation, passions that have continued to guide the Middleton Place Foundation. Thanks to Heningham and Pringle Smith one can recapture a sense of the plantation's elegant past in its no less meaningful present, as it tells its own story and that of its important occupants.[1]

Bulkley Medal

Today Middleton Place, a National Historic Landmark since 1972, is owned and managed by the Middleton Place Foundation, a not-for-profit public trust established in 1974 for the preservation and interpretation of its Gardens, House Museums and Plantation Stableyards. For a hundred and twenty years before the Civil War, throughout the golden eras of indigo, rice and cotton agriculture, the plantation served as the family seat and headquarters for a score of other flourishing plantations. Now in the 21st century, Middleton Place continues to rejuvenate itself with new interpretive initiatives that are accurately documented through ongoing research.

Henry Middleton
1717 – 1784
by Benjamin West

The Middletons were far more
than just landowners and planters.
Men of principal and honor
they were, first and foremost,
servants of the state. They
brought with them from England
a family tradition of political
involvement and took seriously
the responsibility of leadership
expected of them by virtue of
their education and training.

Arthur Middleton
1742 – 1787
by Benjamin West

Henry Middleton
1770 – 1846
by Henry Inman

Williams Middleton
1809 – 1883
by John Stolle

HENRY MIDDLETON (1717-1784)
the founder of Middleton Place,
was the second President of the
First Continental Congress.

—

His son **ARTHUR** (1742-1787)
a dedicated American patriot,
was a signer of the
Declaration of Independence.

—

His grandson **HENRY** (1770-1846)
was Governor of South Carolina,
Congressman, American Minister
to Russia, and an ardent Unionist.

—

His great-grandsons
WILLIAMS (1809-1883)
and **JOHN** (1800-1877),
true to their own political beliefs,
were signers of South Carolina's
Ordinance of Secession in 1860.

—

Their younger brother
EDWARD (1810-1883)
remained loyal to the Union
and served as an officer
in the United States Navy.

The story of the Middletons is integral to South Carolina's evolution and is a microcosm of United States history beginning well before the Revolution. It starts with Henry Middleton's grandfather, Edward Middleton who, with his brother Arthur, emigrated from England to Barbados and from there to South Carolina, eight years after the colonial settlement was established at Charleston.

Genealogical research traces the Carolina family to 1604, to the brothers' grandfather, Richard Middleton of London, who died about 1653. Richard owned a number of properties in and about the city, indicating a certain degree of financial standing. In an age of arranged marriages and dowries, the fact that his daughters and granddaughters married well also underscores the family's status.

For more than twenty years Richard's son Henry was a government official, serving both Charles I and Oliver Cromwell. Henry Middleton (1612-1680) was the father of Edward (1641-1685) and Arthur (1647-1685), the Carolina settlers. Both sons had mercantile interests in Barbados. Edward arrived in Charleston in 1678, and Arthur the following year. In 1680 Edward married Sarah, widow of Richard Fowell, his former business associate. They had one son, named for Edward's brother Arthur, who left no children of his own.[2]

Receiving large grants of land on Goose Creek, not far from the colonial capital, Edward settled a plantation he named The Oaks. As a "Goose Creek man," he typified what one historian has called "that untitled class of landed gentry which…survived the Revolution and formed a distinct and influential element of Charleston society." Though their careers in Carolina were brief (they both died in 1685), from the time of their arrival Edward and Arthur Middleton were part of the ruling elite of the colony. They initiated a continuity of Middleton leadership that lasted through the upheaval of the War Between the States almost two hundred years later. Among other public activities, Edward served as Lords Proprietors deputy.[3]

On Edward's death, his son Arthur (1681-1737) inherited his father's estate. Like his father, Arthur was active in public life. He was President of the Convention that, in 1719, overthrew the Lords Proprietors in favor of being governed by the King. He later served as Governor of South Carolina from 1725 to 1730 under the regal government. Arthur married Sarah Amory and they had three sons who lived to adulthood: William, Henry and Thomas. When Arthur died, his son Henry inherited The Oaks, along with other properties. William, who had built an elegant garden and mansion at Crowfield, eventually returned with his family to settle in England, and Thomas became a merchant-planter in the Beaufort region of South Carolina.[5]

In 1741 Henry Middleton married Mary Williams (1721-1761), only daughter and heiress of John Williams, a wealthy landowner, Justice of the Peace and member of the Assembly. Mary's dowry included his house and the land that was to become known as Middleton Place. It had been in her family since the late 17th century, and here, rather than at The Oaks, they made their home.

Henry Middleton was one of the most influential political leaders of his time and held a number of high offices. He was Speaker of the Commons, Commissioner for Indian Affairs and a member of the Governor's Council until he resigned his seat in 1770 to become a leader of the opposition to British policy. He was chosen to represent South Carolina in the First Continental Congress and on October 22, 1774 was elected its second President. He signed both the Olive Branch Petition appealing to the King of England and an appeal from the American Congress to the citizens of Quebec. Before retiring from public service Henry loaned the fledging state £210,000 South Carolina currency, putting his estate at great financial risk, but clearly reconfirming his devotion to the cause for American independence.

Henry was among the greatest landholders in South Carolina. He owned more than 50,000 acres and approximately 800 slaves. For the last twenty-three years of his life he lived at his earlier home, The Oaks, returning there after the death of his wife Mary in 1761. Henry twice remarried, but his five sons and seven daughters were all children of his first wife. After her death, he relinquished Middleton Place to Arthur, his eldest son and heir.

Arthur Middleton, born at Middleton Place, was educated in England, at Hackney and Trinity Hall, Cambridge. He studied law at London's Middle Temple and traveled extensively in Europe where his taste in classic literature, music and art was developed and refined. Returning to Charleston at the end of 1763, the following summer he married Mary Izard (1747-1814) of Cedar Grove plantation located across the Ashley River from Middleton Place.

Keenly interested in Carolina politics, Arthur Middleton was a more radical thinker than his father. He was a leader of the American Party in South Carolina and one of the

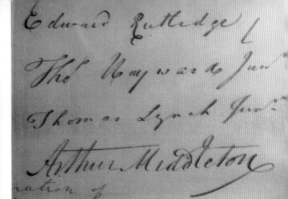

boldest members of the Council of Safety and its Secret Committee. In 1776 he was elected to succeed his father in the Continental Congress and subsequently became a signer of the Declaration of Independence. He was reputed to be quick tempered and impatient. Despite the time he spent in England and notwithstanding his and his wife's many relatives there, his attitude toward British Loyalists could be ruthless. According to archival sources, he approved of the tarring and feathering of several Charleston Loyalists. In August of 1775 he wrote to his friend William Henry Drayton,

> A Mr. Walker[,] Gunner of Fort Johnson[,] had a new suit of Cloaths yesterday without the assistance of a single Taylor – his Crime nothing less than damning us all – during his circumcartation he was stopped at the doors of the principal non-associators & was made to drink damnation to them also not excepting our friend S^r W^m on the Bay.[6]

Later, Middleton and Drayton would design the South Carolina state seal, first used on a document in May of 1777.[7]

During the Revolution, Arthur was active in the defense of Charleston.[8] After the city's fall to the British in 1780, he was sent as a prisoner of war under house arrest to St. Augustine, Florida, until exchanged in July the following year in Philadelphia. He then continued to serve in the Continental Congress. Some years later, John Adams would write of Arthur that, even though they were sometimes on opposite sides of lively debates, "We... parted... without a spark of malice on either side, for he was an honest & generous fellow, with all his zeal in the cause." After his untimely death on January 1, 1787, Arthur was buried at Middleton Place. The plantation then passed to his eldest son, Henry, who had been born in London only 16 years earlier.

The family portrait by Benjamin West shows him as an infant, happily seated between his parents. Well traveled in Europe and his own country, he was to serve for ten years in both houses of the South Carolina state legislature and for a term as Governor. Elected to Congress in 1816, three years later he was appointed by President James Monroe as America's Minister Plenipotentiary to Russia, where he served during the entire decade of the 1820s. On his presidential tour of the South, en route from Charleston to Beaufort and Savannah in early May, 1819, Monroe would stop at "the country seat of the Honorable Henry Middleton, about twelve miles from town," where he would spend the night.

Henry inherited his family's love of the land, developing a lifelong interest in botany. He enlarged and added plantings to the gardens, and was a friend of André Michaux, the famous French botanist who brought many exotic plants to America from France. Family history records that in 1786 Michaux visited Middleton Place, bringing with him the first camellias to be planted in an American garden. The library in the Middleton Place House contains Thomas Walter's *Flora Caroliniana* (1788). In it Henry wrote: "NB. This was Michaux's copy."

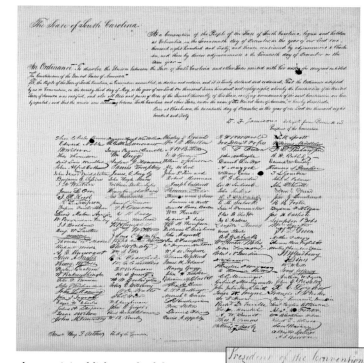

A rare original lithograph of the Ordinance of Secession, by Evans & Cogswell, 1860. The first facsimile edition of the provocative document signed by Williams Middleton and several of his relatives on December 20, 1860, hangs in the first-floor parlor of the Edmondston-Alston House and a copy is in the Library of the Middleton Place House.

At Henry's death, Middleton Place passed to his next-to-youngest son, Williams. Educated in England and Paris, Williams Middleton spent the years 1827 to 1830 in Russia with his father, becoming his personal secretary. After his father's death, he advanced the family's interest in rice culture, carried out agricultural and scientific experiments and enhanced the gardens further with extensive plantings of camellias and azaleas.

Less than a hundred years after the birth of the United States, which his grandfather and great-grandfather had played a role in creating, in December 1860 Williams participated in dissolving the Union by signing South Carolina's Ordinance of Secession. During the ensuing war, Williams supplied the Confederacy with laborers and

materials for the defense of Charleston and Fort Sumter, as well as investing in large amounts of Confederate war bonds. Henry and Arthur's cause had been successful in achieving independence for the United States; the cause Williams championed failed and resulted in the destruction of Middleton Place.[9]

Throughout the generations the gardens and the house made up the fabric of the Middletons' lives. Although not their only residence, it was always, more than any other dwelling, the family's home, the one to which they returned with undisguised pleasure and relief. It was here, as Italian traveler Luigi Castiglioni noted in March, 1786, that Arthur Middleton "having traveled in various parts

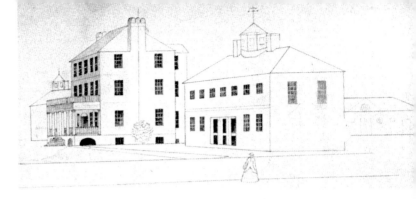

of Europe, has collected a fair quantity of good paintings. His three-story house," he continued, "has the form of an ancient castle…" He adds, "laterally there are two wings that according to the plan were to be joined to the structure in the middle to form an extensive habitation," but there is no evidence that the flankers built in 1755 by the first Henry Middleton were to be physically connected to the house.[10]

Sketch of the Middletons' house and flankers in the 1850s, seen from the north with the stables on the right.

In 1863 Williams Middleton optimistically proposed expanding and redesigning the Middleton Place residential complex.[12]

The south flanker, expanded and restored after the Civil War burning, was the sole survivor of the Great Earthquake of 1886.

In 1839, Governor Henry Middleton's Philadelphia son-in-law described his introduction to Middleton Place,

> …which has certainly more of the signs of civilization than anything I have seen in America. The Pleasure Grounds are very well laid out, very extensive and considering the climate very well kept up. The trees are beautiful – and the number of exotics in the open air quite astonishing. The Establishment too is on a very good footing. The servants are good, very well dressed and just enough of them and everything within the house is as clean and comfortable as one could desire.[11]

The burned out and gutted free-standing walls of the Middleton Place House were felled by earthquake two decades after the Civil War.

Reroofed and enlarged after the war, the restored south flanker (left of ruins) alone survived the Great 1886 Earthquake.[13]

In 1843, Virginian Edmund Ruffin was commissioned to make a survey of South Carolina that included a study of the Ashley River and its plantations. He found that while the riverside offered many beautiful sites for residences and, indeed, was the preferred land in the colonial period, by the time of his study the Ashley River plantations were almost abandoned and rarely inhabited by the owners.

> Along the river there are seen what were once large & costly houses & some even princely establishments, & all (except Middleton Place which its owner still resides on part of the year & maintains in its entire ancient splendor) are either in ruins or seem to be going to ruin.[14]

Richard Yeadon, editor of the *Charleston Daily Courier*, wrote eloquently of Middleton Place in 1857, ten years after Williams Middleton had inherited the property from his father,

> This fine and strongly built brick mansion...is spacious and commodious within, and its interior is adorned with the richest productions of the painter's and sculptor's arts, with [a] gallery of fine family portraits by artists of high fame...in its natural and artificial beauty and elegance, Middleton Place comes nearer, than any place I have seen in America, to the Italian villas, which I visited, or saw, near Rome.[15]

In an earlier article written in 1840 before Governor Middleton's death, Yeadon said,

> Here...we meet with evidence of the taste, wealth and magnificence of colonial times. The mansion... is constructed of common native brick, although finished off in some parts with more polished material, doubtless of English manufacture... Although...considerably more than a century old, it is as substantial and durable as ever, and will probably endure, like the venerable oaks, which shade the adjacent grounds, until the day of final doom, unless deserted, or some uprooting earthquake or tornado shall assign it a shorter term.[16]

"Until the day of final doom..." Yeadon could scarcely have known how ironically prophetic his words would be. Twenty-five years after his article appeared, the end of the Civil War found the buildings at Middleton Place burned and looted, the once-splendid house only a shell. Yet to come was the "uprooting earthquake" that felled the gutted walls, and the many devastating storms and hurricanes that compounded the ruin.

In 1865 a detachment of the 56th New York Volunteers occupied Middleton Place. On February 22nd, the house and its flankers were ransacked and put to the torch, the ground strewn with books, paintings and other family treasures. The place was in total ruin.[17]

Later, the south flanker, least ravaged by the vandalism, was roofed over and strengthened and somewhat expanded to provide a home for the Middleton family. After the August 1886 earthquake, it alone remained standing. Brick upon brick, the charred ruins of the main house and north flanker tumbled into piles of rubble, while gaping holes appeared in the terraces and lakes were sucked dry. Nevertheless, Middleton Place endured. Though damaged, the heart of Middleton Place, its gardens, remained essentially intact.

With financial help from his sister, Eliza Middleton Fisher of Philadelphia, and with some revenue from phosphate mining, Williams Middleton managed to hold on to the family plantation. While despairing at times of being able to repair and maintain what generation after generation viewed as an historic legacy, family members recognized their obligation to preserve the property of their ancestors.

It would take much labor and time, but their ambition eventually would be fulfilled. Imbued with an ethic of preservation and stewardship, family descendants continue to embrace responsibility for the well-being of their ancestral home. And so today, once again, people can visit Middleton Place and appreciate its historic importance.

The combination of the Civil War and earthquake destruction caused garden maintenance to be neglected almost totally until Heningham and Pringle Smith moved to Middleton Place in the second quarter of the 20th century to begin fifteen years of intense landscape restoration.

In Colonial times, waterways served as highways for Low Country planters traveling back and forth to Charleston. As on many plantations, the house at Middleton Place was built facing the river, and there was a dock at the foot of the gardens to accommodate the plantation schooners that carried passengers and freight to and from town. The visitor arriving by boat was greeted by the sight of undulating green terraces stretching up the bluff to the house and its two flanking wings. One can imagine a waiting carriage that would carry the new arrival and his baggage past the twin lakes shaped like butterfly wings and the spring house – later to become the plantation's chapel – and up the roadway around to the gentlemen's guest quarters in the south flanker.

The route by land was over a road that followed part of an ancient Cherokee trail, winding through spreading live oaks festooned with gray Spanish moss, ancestors perhaps of those moss-garlanded trees that, despite the encroachment of modern development, still line parts of the highway. Even well into the 1900s and the age of automobiles, the narrow dirt road was frequently impassable, and a certain amount of horse and buggy, as well as boat traffic, continued through the first two or three decades of the 20th century.

Today's visitors enter Middleton Place from the Ashley River Road (SC Highway 61). Beyond the main gate an imposing expanse of open greensward, bordered by moss-trimmed live oaks and pierced-brick fencing, spreads out over twelve acres. Sheep graze contentedly, helping crop the grass as in centuries past, while bright-plumaged peacocks add exotic color. The very elegance and scale of the approach suggest there is much splendor yet to see.

As the visitor steps from the parking area through the Portal into the Gardens, the present-day world is left behind. Just ahead is the Reflection Pool, with its rank of towering southern magnolias. Planted with careful precision, at certain times of day they cast their shadows on the water in such a way as to suggest an ordered row of majestic

columns. Tidy allées of camellias and specimen trees lead the visitor deeper into the Gardens, each discovered vista lovelier than the last. Past the family tomb, nestled in a shadowy bosquet, one glimpses the ruins of the house and its north flanker, as well as the present House Museum, originally the flanking dependency to the south.

The first breathtaking view comes as one climbs the steps and passes through the iron gates into the ruins of the family house. The gates open onto a brick walk laid where once the center hall was located, and from this commanding site landscaped gardens and terraced lawns stretch down to the river below. It is easy to understand why this riverside spot was selected for the plantation residence.

The view eastward from the head of the terraces looking between the Butterfly Lakes and down the Ashley River is reminiscent of the view from the Palace at Versailles looking down the Grand Canal. Henry Middleton borrowed the natural course of the Ashley River to provide his mile-long vista, while Louis XIV had to underwrite the considerable expense of having Le Nôtre build the similarly sized Grand Canal and have it supplied with adequate water.

The house was built by Mary Williams' father during the years 1705 and 1706, some 35 years before the gardens were laid out following her marriage to Henry Middleton. John Williams built his sturdy brick house perfectly sited on a bluff overlooking the Ashley River. In 1755, with the size of his own family increasing, Henry added the two flanking buildings on either side, integrated with his garden design. In the one to the north were a conservatory and library that eventually held some 10,000 volumes; the plantation's offices and gentlemen's guest quarters were in the flanker to the south. About 1795 the French Duke de la Rochefoucault-Liancourt observed, "The outbuildings,

It is fortuitous that John Williams had sited his early 18th century house perfectly aligned with a natural stretch of the Ashley River so that, 35 years later, his son-in-law could use that alignment as the main axis of his garden plan. From the top of the Greensward circle (lower right above) the main axis runs through the ruins of the house, across the parterre, down the terraces and between the Butterfly Lakes to join the river.

such as kitchen, wash-house, and offices, are very capacious. The ensemble of these buildings calls to recollection the ancient English country seats." [18]

But before he added the flankers to his house, Henry Middleton had begun creating his noble gardens. The gardens that he envisioned and began to create in 1741 reflect the grand classic style that remained in vogue in Europe and England into the early part of the 18th century.

Perhaps a certain prideful arrogance encouraged him in the elaborate embellishment of his new family seat. Maybe he wished to show his English cousins that people in the American colonies could live as elegantly as those in the mother country. It has also been suggested that he sought to outdo his older brother William, whose spectacular 1735 Crowfield plantation garden was rapturously described in 1743 by Eliza Lucas Pinckney. [19]

In any case, Henry was a pioneer in American gardening. A garden as large as the one Henry conceived was, in itself, a bold venture unlike any other in America at that time. It was a garden landscaped with formal symmetry following the principles codified by the French landscape architect, André Le Nôtre. The superb master of garden design laid out Vaux-le-Vicomte and Louis XIV's gardens at the Palace of Versailles, as well as many other great gardens. Le Nôtre died in 1700, but his followers continued his work and variations of his classical themes were echoed far and wide in the gardens of early 18th century Europe.

Great attention was paid to woods and water. The pattern was a central uninterrupted vista, first over parterres to a dividing pathway, continuing on over a geometric sheet of water, through regularly planted woodland, the vista ending in a narrowing remote forest view. Walks, straight and triangulated, were cut through the woods. Allées

were planted with trees and shrubs, trimmed to appear as green walls and partitioning off small galleries, green arbors and bowling greens. There were ornamental canals, designed with mathematical precision, sundials, expansive vistas and statues placed at strategic viewpoints. Grassy ramps were preferred to stairways. The gentle slopes, the soft imperceptible transitions, were more pleasing to the eye and more comfortable for walking. And there were surprises at every turn.

At Middleton Place, the site of the house and the fall of the land suited Henry's landscaping purpose ideally; his appraising eye appreciated the incomparable view of the river. Extended vistas in the Carolina Low Country were usually flat, across great expanses of river and marsh. The view at Middleton Place was an exception. The house stood on high land some forty feet above the river which flowed around the bluff, into a gentle S-curve, turning and forming a wide vista extending for a mile over the tidal water.

The garden design was a superb exercise in logic and geometry, perfectly adapted to the contours of the land. His English gardener, George Newman, may have helped him lay out what

Near the Middleton Oak (lower left) paths radiate like spokes from the sundial in the center of the circular Rose Garden to reach out to the Octagonal Garden (upper left), the Inner Gardens (right), and the Secret Gardens (above). The Reflection Pool is just out of the photograph, as is the Mount.

historian Samuel Gaillard Stoney called, "the premier garden of the thirteen colonies," and the Garden Club of America labeled "the most important and interesting garden in America." The Duke de la Rochefoucault had earlier noted that, "the river, which flows in a circuitous course…forms here a wide, beautiful canal, pointing straight to the house" adding, "the garden is beautiful."[20]

Henry used the east-west axis as a base from which to triangulate his bold garden plan, mainly to the north, with perfect mathematical balance, and to organize a variety of geometrical garden rooms and spaces. The main axis runs west to east straight from the gates on the highway, through the center of the house, down the middle of the curving terraces and between the Butterfly Lakes, to follow the course of the river until it disappears into the wilderness beyond the distant marsh.

The formal garden, based on a large right isosceles triangle that organizes along its hypotenuse the major garden spaces in varying geometric shapes, lies mostly north and west of the house and is divided by parallel and perpendicular paths and allées. The allées, trimmed now to green walls, lead from one axis to another, partitioning off a series of small enclosed garden rooms and periodically affording unexpected views of river, marsh and woodland. It is fortunate and important that the main axis runs from due east to due west: thus producing, a couple of hours before sunset, dramatic shadow-sculptured definition for the terraces.

The dotted lines show that if the large garden-organizing triangle is flipped over to the south, it engages the Plantation Stableyards. And if the thus-formed double triangle is flipped westward from its 90° angle at the head of the terraces, that angle lands at the entrance gate on the Ashley River Road. Under the influence of Descartes and Le Nôtre, the Middletons were all about precise geometric engineering.

The garden is set off from the forest to the west and north, respectively, by the spring-fed Reflection Pool, where swans sail majestically, and the Azalea Pool perpendicular to it. These pools were similarly rectangular in shape, but the Azalea Pool has eroded into freer contours. Beside and below the Azalea Pool, the river forms a natural boundary for the gardens to the east. The Mill Pond was dammed up in the mid 19th century when the Mill was built, both for practical purposes and perhaps also as a garden folly. The pond was originally a creek that defined the southern boundary of the garden. Journalist Richard Yeadon commented on the "neat" mill in 1857, that it was a "real acquisition to the place, and convenience to the neighborhood."[21]

After the creek on the south side of the original
garden was dammed up, it created a handsome
body of water that not only supplied power for the
Mill's turbine, but brought water nearer to the
Spring House and Plantation Chapel. It also allows
reflections of the thousands of azaleas planted on the
hillside to the south in the 1930s.

At the same time he built the Mill, Williams added an upper room to the spring house dairy. In the late 1990s research at the Historical Society of Pennsylvania turned up a letter from Williams to his brother-in-law in Philadelphia written in March 1851.

> I believe I told you that I had built a pretty good room with a vaulted ceiling over the dairy with the intention of placing a billiard table in it one of these days. This has been converted into a Chapel by particular request, & the neighborhood Parson is at this moment holding forth there in full swing to a large & fashionable congregation of all colors.[22]

The Plantation Chapel, like the Slave Cemetery, is now a stop on the African American Focus Tour. Both, like the tour itself, are examples of modern initiatives resulting from extensive research and documentation.

The first of the small gardens entered near the house is a sunken Octagonal Garden. Here, late afternoons, when the house shut off the sun, gentlemen played at bowls, while ladies watched from the surrounding grassy terraces. Next in line is a wheel-shaped Sundial Garden with triangular beds of old roses first propagated in the 18th and 19th centuries. Beyond the Sundial Garden are the remains of the Mount which originally was higher and may have had a small pavilion atop overlooking the gardens and the river.

To the west of the Octagonal Garden and to the south of the Sundial Garden, lies the Bosquet, a wilderness area and a component of the André Le Nôtre garden lexicon. It provides contrast and dynamic tension between the natural and the formal garden spaces. And it echoes the larger counterpoint that exists when looking across the Ashley River to the natural riverscape, which gives a dramatic contrast to the highly refined and carefully designed formal gardens. The Bosquet also provides an ideal burial ground and appropriately contains the family tomb.

Henry would be pleased to see that the framework of his great garden remains intact. And he would be delighted that, in modern times of ever-encroaching suburban development, the Middleton Place Foundation has succeeded in securing conservation easements on the entire two miles of riverscape on the east side of the Ashley River. Instead of houses looming over modern docks extending into the river, the historic natural surroundings seen from the garden are now happily preserved in perpetuity.

Middleton family tomb in the Bosquet.

While gardens do evolve over time, the original plan dating from the second quarter of the 18th century has been strictly adhered to by Henry Middleton's descendants. Summer annuals and perennials have been added with broad brushstrokes to extend colorful blooming year round. The sensitive new plantings are fully respectful of the original bones, the scale and texture and character of the original garden. That being said, it must be remembered that the original garden was begun almost 50 years before the now iconic *Camellia japonica* was introduced and a full century before the *Azalea indica* was added.

It is interesting to note further that, when the romantic movement became dominant, the gardens at Middleton Place were not remade as were many European gardens, but were rather simply expanded – to the north with the inclusion of the Cypress Lake and to the south with the naturally shaped Mill Pond and hillside beyond it – adding new romantic elements, all the while preserving the venerable formal gardens. The result is that Middleton Place survives into the 21st century embracing both the formal and the informal, the man-made and the natural, the classical and the romantic.

One of the many paths that have become tunnels of camellias.

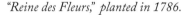

"Reine des Fleurs," planted in 1786.

Tea rose, "Marie van Houtte"

Azalea indica, "President Clay"

Hydrangea, "Hortensia"

Camellia, "Alba Plena"

Today plants that were once shrubs have become tree-sized; young trees have grown to giants. Predominant among the trees is the live oak *(Quercus virginiana)*. For Andreas Feininger, who came to Middleton Place for his live oak photographs, it is the "tree of trees." He saw them in all their glory. The Middleton Oak, a monarch among them, is perhaps a thousand years old. In his book *Trees* (1968) Feininger wrote of live oaks:

> No other tree combines as many virtues with fewer faults...the most beautiful, majestic, yet friendliest of all trees, the tree which as far as humans are concerned is the most rewarding, not in terms of lumber and cash, but in the creation of an atmosphere of comfort, well-being and peace.

The southern magnolia *(Magnolia grandiflora)* is another conspicuous tree, one that Alexander Garden, a botanist and physician in Charleston, described in 1757 as "the finest and most superb evergreen tree that this earth produced."

The four camellia japonicas that André Michaux brought to Middleton Place in 1786 were planted at the four corners of the Parterre. The *"Reine des Fleurs"* still survives, and scions of the original plantings continue to flourish. In the 1940s and 1950s the Middleton Place Nursery directed by the Smiths' daughter, Josephine, propagated great-grandchildren of the first camellias, seedling mutations resulting in new varieties that flourish throughout the Gardens. They are showcased in the New Camellia Garden established by her between the Azalea Pool and the Cypress Lake. Numerous varieties of camellias line the allées in the formal garden. At the height of bloom green tunnels are festooned with flowers and the pathways strewn with a rich carpet of fallen petals.

The Middleton Oak, as it appeared before 2008, with a trunk circumference of some 34 feet and limb spread of 131 feet.

The great oak lost nearly half of its major branches in April 2008, but continues to thrive.

Non-domesticated residents at Middleton Place include the Bald Eagle, Tricolored Heron, White Ibis and American Alligator.

André Michaux also introduced the "Chinese azalea," but they were largely ignored as garden ornamentals.[23] A half century later, during Williams Middleton's lifetime, the first azaleas were planted at Middleton Place. Now the glory of springtime, there are many varieties blooming in the Gardens.

Antique bronze Crane and hillside of azaleas.

Other shrubs widely planted are the anise, both Japanese and native *(Ilicium parviflorum and floridanum),* tea olive *(Osmanthus fragrans),* mountain laurel *(Kalmia latifolia)* and Daphne odora *(Thymelaeceae).* Among the trees are pines (mostly *Pinus taeda),* and white oak *(Quercus alba),* southern red cedar *(Juniperus silicicola),* bald cypress *(Taxodium distichum),* tulip tree *(Liriodendrum tulipifera),* beech *(Fagus grandiflora),* pecan *(Carya illinoensis),* hickory *(Carya pallidal),* redbud *(Cercis canadensis),* American holly *(Ilex opaca)* and buckeye *(Hippocastanaceae).*

There is color in the Gardens the year round. Many varieties of camellias begin to bloom in November and are at their height in February and March. Before the camellias are quite finished, azaleas begin blooming. The hillside above the mill pond, planted in the early 1930s with 35,000 azaleas of many varieties, is ablaze with color.

Dogwood *(Cornus florida),* Cherokee rose *(Rosa laevigata),* wisteria *(Wisteria floribunda)* and Confederate Jasmine *(Trachelospermium jasminoides)* join in the carnival. Springtime at Middleton Place is a heady time. "Old-fashioned" flowers have not been forgotten. Earlier in the year, daffodils *(Narcissus)* and snowdrops *(Galanthus)* add color to the hillside above the sloping banks of the rice fields; native atamasco lilies *(Zephyranthes atamasco)* open their single white flowers around the Cypress Lake; pansies *(Viola tricolor hortenses)* and tulips *(Tulipa)* bloom in the Octagonal Garden and along the main parterre.

Other historic plants, notably tea roses *(Rosaceae)* and china roses *(Hibiscus rosa sinensis)* in the Sundial Garden, as well as classic annuals, bloom in the borders from May until late summer, as do vines, flowering trees and shrubs such as kalmia *(Kalmia latifolia)* and gardenia *(Gardenia jasminoides).* The Magnolias open their great saucerlike ivory flowers in May and June, and crape myrtle trees *(Lagerstroemia indica)* also add colorful flowering.

Marble nude seen from the Middleton Place Restaurant.

"Autumn," one of The Four Seasons in a secret garden.

19th century Italian musical putti play gleefully near the Middleton Oak.

In addition to the 1810 marble Wood Nymph by Rudolph Schadow overlooking the Azalea Pool, fine marble statues of the Four Seasons have been appropriately placed in the corners of the Large Secret Garden. Nineteenth-century Italian musical putti guard a pathway near the Rose Garden and the Middleton Oak. A bronze crane and a marble nude are visible from the Middleton Place Restaurant.

It was probably the utter desolation of the land after the War Between the States that saved the gardens. They were relatively untouched and unharmed, except for the rampant growth that claimed them. So dense was the growth in the garden, turned into "more or less a wilderness," that Heningham Smith had to get down on hands and knees and find the bricks lining the paths to determine where they went and when they made a turn.

During the period of neglect, a "Little Gray Lady" was often reported moving about in the twilight, through the ruins or out on what remained of the terraces, or picking her way through tangled brush. But once the restoration of the garden was well underway the "Little Gray Lady" disappeared, thankfully never to be seen again.

Schadow's 1810 Wood Nymph or Sandalbinder (detail of statue on page 35).

Archival material from the Revolutionary era.[24]

Being ever further enhanced in recent years, the surviving south flanker of the 18th century residential complex at Middleton Place has become an exceptionally important house museum, important for two reasons. First, in its eight rooms and hallways are displayed beautiful objects of extremely high quality: portraits by Benjamin West, Thomas Sully, Rembrandt Peale, Edward Marchant, Charleston made "rice beds" and a Thomas Elfe table, as well as rare volumes of works by Mark Catesby, J. J. Audubon, Humphrey Repton, and Thomas Walters, and a rare early facsimile on silk of the Declaration of Independence.

Second, and perhaps more importantly, virtually all of the objects are Middleton family pieces: the furniture, paintings, silver, porcelain, jewelry, clothing, books, etc., owned and used by generations of Middletons for a century and a half, from the Colonial era through the War Between the States. The history of the Middleton family and the history of America are brought tangibly to life by objects that reflect the interests, the activities, the tastes of people importantly engaged in the early development and subsequent progress of our nation.

Visiting the Middleton Place House, one first enters the Main Room where hang portraits of four generations of Middleton men and women who lived at Middleton Place during the hundred and twenty years before the Civil War. Continental Congress President Henry, Declaration of Independence signer Arthur, Governor/Minister Henry, Ordinance of Secession signer Williams and the wives of the last three men are all here introduced.

Keeping company with the portraits (by Theus and West and Sully and Inman) are Charleston-made side chairs dating from the 1740s, a "breakfast table" made by Charleston's celebrated Thomas Elfe in 1770 and a cabinet full of 18th century silver. From trays to sauce boats, cruets to wine labels and coasters, almost all the silver pieces bear the Middleton crest or coat of arms.

Williams' wife Susan Pringle Smith Middleton by Thomas Sully.

The cabinet next to Susan's portrait in the Main Room contains English silver all acquired in London by Arthur and Mary Middleton in the third quarter of the 18th century, including a set of footed trays made by Robert Rogers.

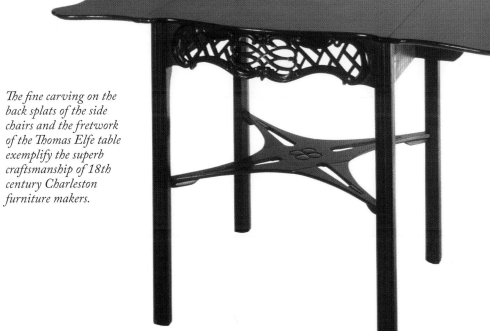

The fine carving on the back splats of the side chairs and the fretwork of the Thomas Elfe table exemplify the superb craftsmanship of 18th century Charleston furniture makers.

Henry Middleton Rutledge

English silver all bearing the Middleton arms or crest, clockwise: a 1724 tankard that belonged to Governor Arthur Middleton (the signer's grandfather), an 1815 Middleton bread basket that descended through intermarriage with the Cadwalader family, a 1766 two-handled loving cup (16½ inches tall) and one of the eight small baskets from the Middletons' 1771 epergne on the dining table.

In the nearby Dining Room, there is more extraordinary silver, with magnificent 1771 candlesticks surrounding a remarkable 1771 epergne, all of which were bought in London the same year Arthur and Mary Middleton sat to be painted by Benjamin West with their first-born child, son Henry. A portrait by Edward Marchant of Henry's youngest sister, Septima, hangs at one end of the room overlooking the table that belonged to her and her husband, Henry Middleton Rutledge (son of Edward Rutledge, another signer of the Declaration of Independence), whose portrait, attributed to Rembrandt Peale, is at the opposite end of the room.[25]

Over the mantle is a painting of tall ships in the Bay of Naples, that with two other Italian paintings – of nuns returning to their convent on a full-moon night with Mt. Vesuvius glowing in the background and of monks under a grape arbor along the Amalfi Coast – were taken at the end of the Civil War.

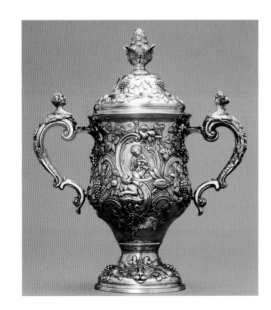

Dr. Henry O. Marcy and two of the paintings he claimed to have "saved from destruction."

All three pictures came back to Middleton Place following a lengthy correspondence in the 1870s between Williams Middleton and Dr. Henry O. Marcy. Marcy had been the medical director of the Union brigade, a detachment of which had burned Middleton Place. In the letters, Marcy said that he

> obtained them with no feeling that I was robbing the owner, but was saving the property from destruction. They cost me $10 each...I had them carefully repaired and framed at the expense of about $30 each...I shall be very willing to return them to you for the amount that they cost me.[26]

Also in the dining room are many pieces of Middleton family porcelain, made in France, England and China before and after the turn of the 19th century and popularly called "Bourbon Sprig." A large soup tureen stands out among them.

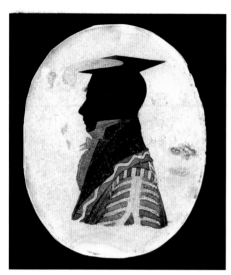

John Izard Middleton at Cambridge, c. 1803.

Tiber River landscape by John Izard Middleton.

John Izard Middleton's "View from my Window at the Hotel Sibella", Tivoli, 1808.

John Izard Middleton's wife, neé Eliza Falconnet, copied by him from her portrait by Thomas Sully.

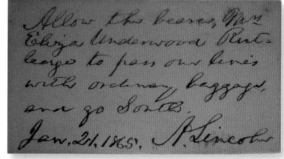

"Laissez-passer" written in 1865 by Abraham Lincoln for the wife of a Middleton descendant. [27]

The Front Hall, west of the Main Room, is dedicated in large part to the youngest son of Arthur and Mary, painter/archeologist John Izard Middleton, whose paintings fill its walls. There is a landscape of the Tiber River flowing through the countryside near Rome, a "View from my Window at the Hotel Sibella, Tivoli, 1808," a copy of Thomas Sully's portrait of Middleton's wife Eliza Falconnet and artist's proofs for his monumental book published in 1812, *Grecian Remains in Italy,* a work that earned him the distinction of being named "America's First Classical Archeologist."[28]

A silhouette of John Izard Middleton is in one of the front hall display cases, together with a myriad of other small objects: important silver pieces, jewelry, miniatures, coins, paper currency, and a note signed "A. Lincoln." There are also antiquities from Italy and Russian treasures that include the tiara worn at Russian court functions in St. Petersburg by Mary Helen Hering Middleton, wife of the Minister, and a miniature copy of a Raphael Madonna signed on the backing paper, "Maria H. Middleton, from Papa, St. Petersburg, 1824." And those, together with a pair of French bronze statues of Voltaire and Rousseau studiously ignoring each other across the mantle, guide visitors into the Empire or Music Room to find objects that mostly date from the second quarter of the 19th century.

The miniature of Raphael's "Madonna of the Garden" given by "Papa" to his eldest daughter Maria, 1824.

Tiara and bracelet worn by Mary Helen Hering Middleton at formal events in St. Petersburg.

French bronze statues of Voltaire and Rousseau.

The Music Room with its fine suite of Philadelphia-made furniture is dominated by a large portrait of Alexander I's younger brother, Nicholas I, the second Czar who reigned while Henry was United States Minister Plenipotentiary to Russia. Here also are several early 19th century masterful copies from French and Italian museums of popular paintings by Raphael, Greuze and Domenichino. Outstanding among them is a miniature on porcelain by Pierre Guérin of Madame Juliette Récamier (who had befriended John Izard Middleton) copied from the famous large portrait by François Guérard. On an easel is a restored Russian painting by Samsonov showing a picture gallery at the Winter Palace in St. Petersburg. The room's many fine objects, that also include a French brass and ormolu gothic clock by Leroy & Fils and an elaborate 19th century American silver tea service, are all appropriately pulled together visually with an Aubusson carpet.

1825 French clock

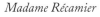

Madame Récamier

On the second floor of the Middleton Place House are two bedrooms, a library and a child's bedroom. The first of the bedrooms, on the right at the top of the stairs, is the south or Winter Bedroom, dressed for the cooler months of the year. Window and bed hangings, as well as upholstery, are all from the same bolt of a documented 18th century French toile, reproduced by Scalamandré. A Charleston rice bed, with foot posts carved to celebrate what had become by the end of the 18th century the most successful of South Carolina's one-crop economies, dominates the room.

At the foot of the bed is a leather trunk with brass fittings that was discovered some years after the Smiths moved to Middleton Place. Black from age and neglect and covered with rotting straw, the tightly sealed trunk had long gone unnoticed. But when opened it proved to be lined with camphor wood, which protected the contents. Inside were silk brocade waistcoats, vests and breeches identified as belonging to Arthur Middleton and his father. Experts who have examined the clothing suggest the gold silk brocade waistcoat and pair of breeches (on the bottom shelf in the photo to the left) are, in fact, those worn by Henry Middleton in his circa 1770 portrait painted by Benjamin West – a rare case of clothing worn in an 18th century portrait still together with that portrait.

The waistcoats and breeches are conserved inside a Charleston-made clothes press standing across the room from a South Carolina desk, on top of which sits a bracket clock made in London circa 1790. Also here in the south bedroom is a sewing box that belonged to a daughter of Henry, Hester Middleton, who was married to Dr. Charles Drayton, a son of John Drayton, the builder of Drayton Hall. Similarly from their marriage is a large Chippendale-style mahogany side chair made in Great Britain in the third quarter of the 18th century. Finally, unusual andirons on a half circle base with a center clef are one of four pairs in the house believed to have been made in London at the turn of the 18th century exclusively for the Charleston market.

Elizabeth Pringle miniature

Pringle, identifies the oval portrait at the head of the bed, copied from it almost four decades later in Paris by Constant-Joseph Brochart. The Robert Smiths were the parents of Susan Pringle Smith (also painted by Sully, her portrait is downstairs in the Main Room, page 41), the wife of Williams Middleton.[29]

At the opposite end of the upstairs hall is the north or Summer Bedroom, shown as it would have been dressed during the warmer months with bed and window hangings replaced by light dimity, reproduced by Scalamandré in the late 20th century. The rice bed, with its headboard removed, would have been pushed out into the room, the mosquito netting dropped and the windows opened wide to allow a breeze to flow through the room. The east and west walls accommodate, respectively, an American bow front chest of drawers and an English chest-on-chest, both from the beginning of the 19th century.

Above the fireplace is a portrait by Thomas Sully of his sister, Elizabeth, who married Henry Middleton Smith, a grandson of the first Henry Middleton. Interestingly Sully, whose initials are on the back, did not depict his sister as flatteringly as he usually did his female sitters. On the mantelpiece are copies of two miniatures that are kept in archival storage. The earlier, by Charles Fraser, is of Robert Smith Jr. (1786-1847), son of Bishop Robert Smith. The accompanying miniature (c. 1820) of his wife, Elizabeth

Between the two bedrooms are a library on the east and a child's bedroom on the west. Notably in the library is a first edition of Mark Catesby's two-volume *Natural History of Carolina, Florida and the Bahama Islands* (1731, 1743). There are also the elephant folios of J. J. Audubon's *Viviparous Quadrupeds of North America* – several lithographs of birds indigenous to South Carolina from his *Birds of America* hang in the upstairs hall – and an engraving on silk of the first facsimile edition of the Declaration of Independence.

Among the few hundred books that have survived from the Middletons' library of more than 10,000 volumes are works by Thomas Walter, Humphrey Repton and Edmund Burke with signatures of Arthur Middleton and his son, Henry. There is a hand-colored "fête book" that records the 1825 funeral procession of Czar Alexander I, presented to Minister Henry Middleton's daughter, Maria, by the German Ambassador, General Dörenberg. There is also an important 18th century map of a Middleton plantation on the Santee River by Charleston's foremost cartographer, James Purcell.

The library contains the hand-colored "fête book" that records the 1825 funeral procession of Czar Alexander I.

Directly across the hall from the Library is a small child's bedroom dating from the post Civil War restoration. The furnishings are therefore late 19th century, including Middleton children's furniture and books and toys and dolls. The room serves to remind us that there were many children who grew up at Middleton Place over the centuries. The Child's Bedroom in today's House Museum was, in fact, used by young Middleton descendants until the last quarter of the 20th century.

Eliza Middleton Fisher

Mary Helen Hering Middleton

Mary Izard Middleton

Thomas Middleton

Paolina Bentivoglio Middleton

Arthur Middleton

The collection of 18th and 19th century objects, with their impeccable Middleton family provenances, came together producing ever increasing enthusiasm over the decades following the opening of the House Museum to the public in 1975. There was, in the beginning, a good base from which to start, established by the legacy of Heningham and Pringle Smith: many pieces of furniture including the rice beds, the Thomas Elfe breakfast table, the Charleston clothes press and the Philadelphia furniture. There were a few of the paintings, important books and some silver. But striving to furnish the House Museum nearly completely with extraordinary and documented Middleton possessions became a multi-faceted effort that has produced, and continues to produce, almost miraculous results.

Early on, the Benjamin West portraits of Henry and Arthur Middleton came on extended loans from England and Philadelphia. Soon thereafter, a small pastel drawing of Williams Middleton's younger sister, Eliza, who married Joshua Francis Fisher, was given to the Foundation, as was a pastel portrait of her mother, Governor Henry Middleton's wife, Mary Helen Hering. And more recently, the handsome portrait attributed to Rembrandt Peale of Henry Middleton Rutledge was given. Over the years fine miniatures of Arthur Middleton's wife, Mary Izard, of his brother, Thomas, of his grandson, Arthur and the latter's wife, the Italian Countess Paolina Bentivoglio Middleton

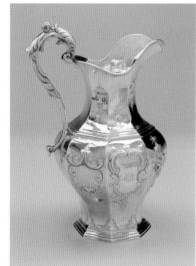

Clockwise: one of the pair of American side chairs (c. 1790) in the Summer Bedroom, one of the four pairs of Middleton candlesticks made by John Carter in 1771, a pitcher and a cup both made in Charleston by John Ewan (c. 1840-50) and a gold locket inscribed "Lisinka from her Julchen." [30]

have similarly enriched the Foundation's collection.

In the late 1970s, an American side chair, originally from a Middleton plantation, came from Washington, DC; and soon thereafter, a matching chair came from Mt. Pleasant, South Carolina. Then the Middleton breakfront (now in the Dining Room) that was made in Salem, Massachusetts by Edmund Johnson (c. 1800) was given to the Foundation by other members of the same family branch. And the dining room table, long residing in Nashville, was sent "home" to Middleton Place by descendants of the Henry Middleton Rutledge family.

Among additions to the important collection of surviving Middleton silver, all eight of the candlesticks listed in the inventory of Arthur Middleton's estate came (as gifts and extended loans) to light warmly the Middleton Place House Museum's Dining Room, some 240 years after they were made in London by John Carter. Less than a month after a coffee pot and tea pot, both bearing the Middleton crest and the makers' mark "Ball, Black & Co." were presented to the Foundation, a cousin of the donor arrived with a stack of receipts, lists, letters, and other papers – not knowing that among them was a receipt from Ball, Black & Co., New York, dated November 13th, 1854, "For 1 Silver Coffee Pot $160 and a silver tea pot $110, totaling $270, with $160 received from Mr. Middleton on account."

The well-documented Middleton silver coffee pot and tea pot made by Ball, Black & Co. in 1854 and given to the Middleton Place Foundation in 2010.

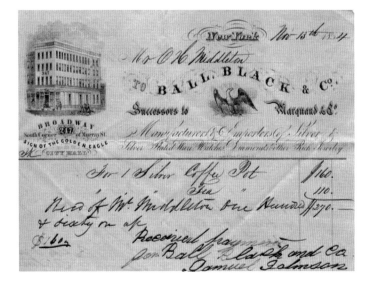

Similar coincidences occur frequently and add excitement to the joy of pieces coming together to broaden and deepen the authenticity of historic interpretation that is brought to life by dedicated staff members and volunteer interpreters. It is the passionate interest and great generosity of Middleton descendants that have preserved vital elements of Middleton Place. And ongoing family stewardship continues to make possible enhanced education about American history through the lens of the Middleton family.

It is perhaps also a uniquely southern story of family members holding on to vestiges of their past and then giving them up to allow a phoenix, once consumed by fire, to rise again. In the 1860s, the South was defeated and subjected to a dramatic reversal of fortune and well-being. As did most families, rich or poor, black or white, descendants of the South Carolina Middletons suffered through a long period of relative poverty exacerbated by political, economic and natural disasters. The Great Earthquake of 1886 provided possibly the most vivid iconographic images of the hard times, that were to last well into the 20th century.

But thanks to a series of virtual miracles, Middleton Place has now survived into its fourth century of unfailing family stewardship. The prospering of this National Historic Landmark would not have happened without the generosity of latter-day supporters of the preservation work of the Middleton Place Foundation. Dedicated descendants and generous benefactors have assured that the microcosm of American history they have helped preserve will remain alive and well in perpetuity.

A slave badge from Mary Izard Middleton's Cedar Grove Plantation.

Throughout the house are pieces that were handled and cared for by the family's African American servants, especially the silver and china and linens. Among a number of objects that speak directly about the enslaved population of Middleton Place are livery buttons marked with the family crest, a municipally issued slave badge that permitted an enslaved servant to be "hired out" and legally employed in Charleston, a cotton sack embroidered with a poignant message and roughly finished Edgefield pots made and used by enslaved Africans.

But it is the Plantation Stableyards that presents the strongest evidence and clearest interpretation of the enslaved African American members of the extended Middleton Place family.

Livery buttons bearing the Middleton family crest.

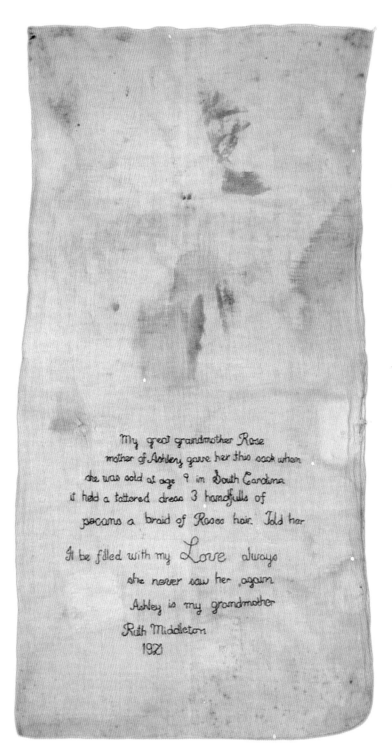

My great grandmother Rose
mother of Ashley gave her this sack when
she was sold at age 9 in South Carolina
it held a tattered dress 3 handfulls of
pecans a braid of Roses hair. Told her
It be filled with my *Love* always
she never saw her again
Ashley is my grandmother
Ruth Middleton
1921

The Plantation Stableyards have been rejuvenated with the installation of period-correct fencing. Black locust posts and rails, "eleven feet long and heavy," define enclosures for large animals of historic breeds: water buffalo first brought from Constantinople to work in the rice fields at Middleton Place in the 1850s, a Jersey cow that is milked twice daily and driving horses that are used today much as they would have been by the Middletons hundreds of years ago. Guinea hogs, like ones in the "hog crawl," were imported from West Africa over two hundred years ago and were common on Low Country plantations until replaced by modern breeds.

Follow the lanes ahead to the west, then north to Eliza's House, to learn about the history of slavery at Middleton Place "beyond the fields." Nearby are pens for Gulf Coast sheep, believed to have been here in the 18th and 19th centuries, and Cashmere goats, introduced in the 1850s by Williams Middleton, who sent their "hair" to France "to have it manufactured by way of curiosity." Finally, continue on between the barn and the blacksmith shop to visit with a potter, a carpenter / cooper, a spinner / weaver and others who interpret the self-sustaining plantation activities of yesteryear.

Beyond the elegant façade of America's oldest landscaped gardens and the Middleton Place house was constant work activity. Crops were sown and harvested, domestic animals were husbanded. Hinges and nails, boards and shingles, soap, candles and yarn were made by hand by enslaved Africans. In 1970, when Charleston celebrated the tricentennial of its founding, the Middleton Place barn and sheds and paddocks, that had been reconstructed early in the 20th century, were opened to the public to increase understanding of 18th and 19th century plantation life.

Most visitors today enter the Plantation Stableyards by walking up from the bridge over the Mill Pond and into the enclosures south and east of the buildings. To the right, just before the fence gate, is an old slave cemetery where three pre Civil War gravestones survive. Dating from 1851 and 1859, they had been overtaken by the property-wide neglect and were only uncovered in the mid 20th century. Above and to the right of these markers are the Stableyards buildings in which the traditional hand-worked trades are demonstrated.

In 2010, forty years after the opening of the Plantation Stableyards, grants made possible completing a rejuvenation project to install period-correct fencing. Black Locust posts and rails, "eleven feet long and heavy,"[31] define areas for large animals of historic breeds: water buffalo first brought from Constantinople by Williams Middleton to work in the rice fields at Middleton Place in the 1850s; early breeds of cows that are milked twice daily; and driving horses that are worked much as they would have been for the Middletons hundreds of years ago. Guinea hogs, like the ones in the "hog crawl," were imported from West Africa over two hundred years ago and were common on Low Country plantations until replaced by modern breeds.

One follows the lanes ahead to the west, then north to Eliza's House, to learn about the history of slavery at Middleton Place "beyond the fields." Along the route are enclosures for the Stableyards animal population interspersed with demonstration plantings of historic crops such as sugar cane and cotton. The sugar cane is milled in the fall at harvest time, as a mule powers the sugar cane press from which juice is brought to a boil in the nearby cauldron to produce molasses. At the end of the lanes and behind Eliza's House is the poultry yard and fowl house, home to a variety of historic breeds of hens. The front is screened and indented so that children can get a close view of the hens in their laying boxes.

Eliza's House, at the western end of the Stableyards, is named for its last resident, Eliza Leach, who lived there for decades through the 1980s until her death at age 94. Soon thereafter, the vernacular two-family freedman's house was restored to its original appearance. Modern electricity and plumbing were removed, as were the sash windows and interior wallpaper. The two rooms on the western side of the building were furnished to interpret the lives of freedmen. From documents in the Foundation's archives, researchers learned about Ned and Chloe who had moved into the small house when it was first built about 1870. Originally built where the Middleton Place Restaurant is today, Eliza's House was relocated beyond the Stableyards buildings when the Smiths began rescuing Middleton Place in the second quarter of the 20th century.

Opened in 1991, Eliza's House became a focal point for African American research and interpretation and was well received by an increasingly interested visiting public. One room is furnished as Ned and Chloe's bedroom, the other as shelter for living, eating and working. Outdoor spaces in the "swept yard" were designated for social gathering in the front, cooking and washing to the rear.

While visitors found the freedmen's story interesting and educational, the question soon surfaced: "What about slavery at Middleton Place?"

In response to that repeated question, Foundation staff researchers began a decade-long effort to gather and study documentation of the full story of slavery at Middleton Place. In late 2004, the permanent exhibition, "Beyond the Fields" (published in book form in 2008) was opened to complete the interpretive mission of Eliza's House.

After an introductory glimpse into the lives of Ned and Chloe, the visitor learns about the couple's enslaved forebears. Entering the room in the eastern side of Eliza's House, one encounters a panel listing almost 3,000 names of slaves who toiled on a score of Middleton plantations from 1738 to 1865. The extensive research has made possible annotating many of the names with spouses and children, occupations (such as carpenter, cooper, schooner captain, gardener, seamstress, cook) and monetary values taken from estate inventories, plantation lists and other records – in pounds before the American Revolution and in dollars afterwards. Additionally, the first room focuses on the African experience of those who became enslaved, their way of life prior to being captured and then the horrors of incarceration and the Middle Passage shipment to Charleston.

The second room celebrates the contributions of enslaved African Americans and freed people to the well-being of Middleton Place. It was they who built Henry Middleton's great gardens and extensive complex of buildings, cared for the white folk in the big house, husbanded the livestock, grew the crops and performed the tasks that are today demonstrated in the Plantation Stableyards. Finally, it was their descendants, like Eliza Leach (and Mary Sheppard and Anna Perry), who in the 20th century were the first interpreters of African American history at Middleton Place.

Wide lanes allow visitors, on foot and in carriages, to traverse the enclosures of the Plantation Stableyards fenced with Black Locust split rails.

The presentation, in its simplicity, is a serious study exhibit that simultaneously produces an authentic feeling of belonging where it is. With its shutters opened to the world around it, Eliza's House looks out through great live oaks to the Greensward manicured by grazing sheep, to the barn and activities in the Plantation Stableyards and to the animals reminiscent of their early plantation antecedents.

Not far away are pens for Gulf Coast sheep, believed to have been here in the 18th and 19th centuries, and Cashmere goats, introduced in the 1850s by Williams Middleton, who sent their "hair" to France "to have it manufactured by way of curiosity." Finally, one continues past the kitchen garden and on between the barn and the blacksmith shop to visit sequentially with a blacksmith, a potter, a carpenter/cooper, a spinner/weaver and others who interpret the self-sustaining plantation activities of yesteryear.

Dyeing yarn

Shearing sheep

Fanning rice

Dipping candles

The Stableyards contain many reminders of day-to-day life on a Low Country plantation. The blacksmith works at his forge, the potter throws clay on a kick wheel, the carpenter/cooper demonstrates his craft and in the spinning and weaving room flax and wool are spun and woven into cloth.

Working in a yoke, water buffalo are trained to pull wagons and sleds.

The main Stableyards buildings stand near the site of the original barns and outbuildings that were burned at the end of the Civil War. The barn itself contains feeding stalls, feed storage bins and a hayloft. Saddles and tack, used to harness horses and oxen and mules, hang from the walls. Tools and implements are displayed in the adjoining buildings: plows, hoes, harrows, seeders, flails, rice hooks and barrels. These are some of the reminders of an era during which the economy of the Carolina Low Country depended on its natural resources and the cultivation and harvesting of crops.

Much of the early wealth of Carolina was derived from forest products. Tar, turpentine and deer hides were shipped from Charleston by plantation owners until rice, indigo and cotton became the money crops. Rice was grown at Middleton Place throughout the 18th and 19th centuries. Water works and dikes were first dug out of inland swamps to create early rice fields. Later, banks and trunks were built to enclose Ashley River marshland that was flooded from fresh water reserves. These tasks were accomplished by hand laborers aided by oxen and mules.

The Stableyards contain many other reminders of day-to-day life on a Low Country plantation. The blacksmith works at his forge, pumping bellows to keep the fire burning hot. Pottery is thrown on a kick wheel, allowing visitors to see a vessel rising into its intended shape from a small mound of clay; historically, coil and pinch pots were made by enslaved Africans for their own use. The carpenter turns chair legs on the great wheel lathe and pares cypress staves and shingles on the shaving horse.

In the spinning and weaving room, flax and wool are spun and woven into cloth. Walnut hulls, indigo and wild berries are used for dyeing the thread and yarn. Middleton Place sheep earn their keep by helping to maintain a trim and neat lawn between the entrance gates and the House. They also supply much of the wool used for spinning and weaving.

A carriage enters the bamboo forest as visitors are shown the plantation much as would have happened in centuries past.

The hominy mill found on nearly every plantation is still used to grind shelled corn into grits and corn meal. Those who try to keep the hand-operated millstone turning soon discover that both strength and perseverance are demanded. Nearby, beeswax or bayberry wax is melted in a large cauldron over an open fire and candles are dipped again and again until they are large enough for use. Finer candles were molded in tin frames, a far more time-consuming process.

The plantation bell no longer summons the field hands or sounds alarms. Nor do carriages in the carriage house travel the old River Road from Middleton Place to Charleston. But these, like the hand-made tools and implements, are reminders of the days when men, women and children lived close to the land, when a trip to Charleston was a day's journey and there was no running water, no electricity, no telephone, no internet and no nearby store.

Carriages today take visitors around the periphery of the Gardens, through the Bamboo Forest and out onto a rice field bank to see a variety of both resident and migratory birds. The trip provides an experience similar to that of guests over the centuries being shown highlights of the plantation by members of the Middleton family.

Middleton Place provides the opportunity to experience authentically interpreted 18th and 19th century life, fulfilling the mission of the Middleton Place Foundation to ensure the preservation of this important National Historic Landmark. North America's oldest landscaped gardens have been able to meet the tests of almost three hundred years, surviving the ravages of both man-made and natural disasters. Middleton Place has not recently been threatened by pillaging and burning, nor by earthquakes, but rather by the encroachment of development along the Ashley River and the Ashley River Road.

Following a hiatus of nearly a century and a half, "Carolina Gold" rice is once again being grown at Middleton Place. On a daily "task" portion of the Garden Rice Field, a boardwalk out into the field allows visitors to become intimate with the historic crop that once brought great wealth to South Carolina planters. In the Mill nearby, adding to the African American Focus tour, Alice Ravenel Huger Smith watercolors depict the sequential stages of rice cultivation in the 1850s.

The preservation of the riverscape, an essential part of the environment of "the most important and interesting garden in America," has been accomplished with the establishment of conservation easements protecting some two miles of riverscape within the Landmark's viewshed. The Foundation has also acquired extensive easements along the Ashley River Road. And, with the participation of neighboring landowners, conservation easements now protect a majority of the Historic Ashley River Plantation District, of which the Middleton Place Woodlands across the highway from the National Historic Landmark is an important part. The monitoring and enforcement of the various easements will be a continuing responsibility for future generations of the Foundation's trustees and land stewards.

With vigilance, Middleton Place will always remain a place to step back in time, a place to walk garden paths now more than a quarter of a millennium old and visualize, with serenity, life of a bygone era.

1. Pringle Smith's father, Henry Augustus Middleton Smith (1853 – 1924) was also responsible for rescuing Middleton Place, briefly assuming its ownership in order to resolve certain financial and legal problems. Named a Federal Judge by President William Howard Taft, H. A. M. Smith was a distinguished jurist as well as a respected South Carolina historian. His three volumes of articles published by the South Carolina Historical Society *(The Baronies of South Carolina, Cities and Towns of Early South Carolina,* and *Rivers and Regions of Early South Carolina)* are standard sources for researchers.

2. In 1637 Henry Middleton was named Keeper of Garden Doors "for life" at the royal residence of Whitehall. One year later he was appointed by Charles I as Sergeant at Arms, carrying the ceremonial mace, a position he would retain under Oliver Cromwell. *Survey of London*, Montagu H. Cox and Philip Norman, editors. B.T. Batsford, Ltd., 1930. *London Survey,* R. H. W. Sheppard, editor. Athlone Press, 1983.

3. Edward Middleton was also a member of the Grand Council and an Assistant Justice. His brother Arthur was likewise a member of the Grand Council and Lords Proprietors Deputy. Edward's son Arthur (1681-1737) was Naval Officer for South Carolina, Commissioner of Indian Affairs, and Proprietors Deputy. Langdon Cheves, "Middleton of South Carolina." *South Carolina Historical Society Magazine*, Vol I, No. 3, July 1900.

4. Original sketch by Countess Paolina Bentivoglio, circa 1842; color added by Eliza Chrystie. Paolina was the Italian wife of Arthur Middleton, eldest son of Governor Henry Middleton; the sketch was a gift from the Italian branch of the Middleton family.

5. William Middleton (1710-1775) served in the South Carolina Commons and was appointed to the Royal Council. Thomas Middleton (1719-1766) also served in the Commons, was Justice of the Peace and Colonel in the Carolina Regiment, taking part in the campaign against the Cherokees. Cheves, op cit.

6. "A new suit of clothes…" is Arthur Middleton's euphemism for tar-and-feathering. Middleton and Drayton were equally condemning of "non-associators," those Carolinians who refused to side with the "associators," i.e., the revolutionaries. "Sʳ Wᵐ on the Bay": Sir William Campbell was the last Royal Governor of South Carolina who, at the time Middleton wrote, had taken refuge on a British Navy vessel in Charleston's harbor. Arthur Middleton to William Henry Drayton, August 12, 1775. Middleton Place Archives.

7. South Carolina's great seal was a round, double sided device of wax with separate designs on the obverse (front) and reverse (back), attached to documents by a ribbon or cord. This proving unwieldy, it was soon revised to be a one-sided seal showing both designs in smaller, separate ovals. The seal in its original form was last used on the 1860 Ordinance of Secession. State Seal article by David C. Heisser, *The South Carolina Encyclopedia*, Walter Edgar, editor. University of South Carolina Press, 2006.

8. Arthur Middleton's presence with the colonial militia during the 1779 British invasion of South Carolina led by General Prevost, is established by his brother-in-law Charles Cotesworth Pinckney's letter of May 26, 1779 to his wife Sarah. Pinckney Family Letters, Library of Congress.

9. The Middleton Place Archives contain Confederate States of America bonds amounting to $66,000. One bond alone is for $30,000. If these bonds had been issued in United States dollars instead of Confederate currency, Williams Middleton's investment would be valued at $1,790,000 in 2010 dollars. *www.measuringworth.com*

10. *Voyage to the United States of North America in the Years 1785-86-87.* Luigi Castiglioni, Milan, 1790.

11. J. Francis Fisher to George Harrison, 28 March, 1839. Cadwalader Collection, Historical Society of Pennsylvania.

12. During the Civil War Williams Middleton made great plans for remodeling the buildings at Middleton Place in a Flemish style. Thwarted by the outcome of the war, when he restored the south flanker in 1869-70 for use as his residence he did manage to incorporate Flemish gable ends as a decorative feature. In the 1930s when the Smiths remodeled the stableyard buildings, their architect Bancel LaFarge referenced those gables in his design for the new stables. Middleton Place Foundation Archives.

13. Stereographs, circa 1875, by B. W. Kilburn, published by Kilburn Brothers, Littleton, N.H.

14. *Agriculture, Geology and Society in Antebellum South Carolina: The Private Diary of Edmund Ruffin, 1843*, William M. Mathew, editor. University of Georgia Press, 1992 .

15. *The Charleston Daily Courier* Tuesday April 21, 1857.

16. *The Charleston Courier* Saturday March 7, 1840.

17. "Thursday Feb. 23 1865:…Everything was in confusion. The house was strewed with articles and all about the grounds things were scattered…Soon found my way to the Library, which I think was the largest and most select I have ever seen…I sickened at the thought of such pillage as was about to occur and retired begging [Major Smith] whatever else he might do, to spare the library." Transcript of Dr. Henry Orlando Marcy's diary courtesy of Henry O. Marcy IV. Middleton Place Archives.

"I have just returned home, and visited St. Andrew's and St. George's Parishes or what remains of them. Everything is completely destroyed, there are but two houses left on our side [of the river]…I visited your place, but I suppose you may have heard of what has happened, it is almost too shocking for me to relate… I went over on the other side [of the mill pond]… everything is burnt and destroyed, dwelling, outhouses, stable, barn and negro houses, nothing but the ruins… " John Drayton to Williams Middleton, June 2, 1865. Middleton Place Archives.

18. *Travels Through the United States of North America*, the Duke de la Rochefoucault-Liancourt, London, R. Phillips,1799.

19. In a circa 1743 letter to a friend in London, Eliza Lucas described the mile-long approach from the road to the Crowfield house, the pond or "basoun" in the center of a greensward, the long walk on the other side of the house with its grassy plats, serpentine rows of flowers, bowling green, oak grove, "wilderness," fish ponds, mounts, and rice fields "dressed in vivid green." *Plantations of the Carolina Low Country,* Samuel Gaillard Stoney. Carolina Art Association, Revised Edition, 1964.

Not long after visiting Crowfield, Eliza Lucas became Mrs. Charles Pinckney, eventual mother of Thomas and Charles Cotesworth Pinckney and mother-in-law of the latter's wife, Arthur Middleton's sister Sarah.

20. Rochefoucault-Liancourt, op. cit.

21. *The Charleston Daily Courier,* Tuesday April 21, 1857.

22. Williams Middleton, Middleton Place, to J. Francis Fisher, Philadelphia, March 9, 1851. Pennsylvania Historical Society.

23. *André and François André Michaux*, Henry Savage, Jr. and Elizabeth Savage. University Press of Virginia, 1986.

24. 18th and 19th century books and newspapers mentioning the Middletons are included in the large Middleton Place collection of archival material that underscores the Foundation's knowledge and interpretation of the family's history.

25. Henry Middleton Rutledge was also a grandson of Henry Middleton (1717 – 1784), his mother being Arthur Middleton's sister Henrietta.

26. Letter from Dr. Henry Marcy to Williams Middleton, November 7, 1867. Middleton Place Archives.

27. The Lincoln note is a pass that reads: "Allow the bearer Mrs. Eliza Underwood Rutledge to pass our lines with ordinary baggage and go South. A. Lincoln, Jan. 21, 1865." Eliza Rutledge was the daughter-in-law of Septima and Henry Middleton Rutledge, married to their son, Major Arthur Middleton Rutledge. She was returning to Tennessee from Washington where her brother, who fought for the Confederacy, was a prisoner. Their father, Judge Joseph Rogers Underwood, was a former Congressman and United States Senator from Kentucky.

28. In 1885 John Izard Middleton was hailed by Professor Charles Eliot Norton of Harvard as the first American classical archeologist. Langdon Cheves, op. cit. and letters in Middleton Place Foundation Archives.

29. Susan Pringle Smith Middleton's mother was an older sister of Emma Pringle, wife of Charles Alston, thus establishing a close relationship between the Williams Middleton and Charles Alston families. The Alstons' home on Charleston's East Battery, the Edmondston-Alston House, is a house museum of the Middleton Place Foundation.

30. Williams Middleton's sister Eliza and Julia Ward met in Newport, RI and became fast friends; Julia gave Eliza this locket with a snip of her hair as from one red-head to another. Williams and Julia were romantically attached and his family hoped they would marry. However, her father discouraged the match. Instead, she married Samuel Gridley Howe and later became renowned as the author of *The Battle Hymn of the Republic*.

31. Plantation Diary, Henry Augustus Middleton, Jr., South Carolina Historical Society.

The Middleton Place Foundation preserves and interprets its Gardens, House Museum and Plantation Stableyards, as well as a second family related House Museum at 21 East Battery in downtown Charleston, the Edmondston-Alston House. A not-for-profit public trust, the Foundation was established in 1974 to implement the policies of conservation and preservation that guide the day-to-day operations of Middleton Place; it also coordinates interpretive tours of the Gardens, House Museums and Plantation Stableyards, as well as daily Garden Overview Tours and African American Focus Tours. In concert with its preservation, conservation and interpretation mandates, the Foundation works closely with educators and has developed appropriate programs for various levels of study.

Foundation membership helps support the work of the Foundation. Members enjoy numerous benefits, including admission to the Edmondston-Alston House as well as all of Middleton Place; newsletters provide articles of historical interest and up-to-date information. The Foundation welcomes donations, in-kind gifts and loans relevant to its purpose. These, like membership contributions, are tax-deductible to the extent provided by law.

One of the first dwellings built on Charleston's
High Battery, the Edmondston-Alston House
is a gracious example of early 19th-century
commitment to elegance, style and comfort. The
house contains Alston family furniture, silver, books,
paintings and documents that remain in place
much as they have for over 170 years. Both General
Beauregard and General Lee were here in 1861.

Annual Events add festivity to the usual activity in the Gardens, House Museums and Plantation Stableyards. Camellia Walks highlight the burst of color in the Gardens during the winter months, while Civil War and Revolutionary War encampments, Living History Days, a Spring Wine Fest and Easter Eggstravaganza herald warmer weather. Music fills the Gardens during the Spoleto Festival Finale and other occasional concerts. Fall harvest activities are the focus of Plantation Days. Family Yuletide in the Stableyards, a favorite Low Country holiday event, completes the plantation preparations for the Christmas season. "Christmas 1782" is celebrated at Middleton Place with a Grand Illumination, while in Charleston "Christmas 1860" at the Edmondston-Alston House dramatically interprets the last gala holiday season before the beginning of the Civil War.

Middleton Place Restaurant

Located between the Stableyards and the House Museum, the Restaurant specializes in Low Country cuisine of the plantation era. The Restaurant serves lunch daily for visitors to the property and is open for dinner six nights a week. The Pavilion is available for large group functions that are coordinated by Special Group Services managers, who make available a variety of options for corporate events, weddings, and any groups of more than fifteen people.

Museum Shop and Garden Market & Nursery

The Museum Shop offers guests unique plantation-made craft items, books and prints of Low Country interest along with other carefully selected items relating to Middleton Place. The Garden Market and Nursery sells flowers and plants derived from the Middleton Place gardens and offers beverages and quick lunch options. They are both conveniently located in the Visitor Center Parking area.

The Inn at Middleton Place

A recipient of the American Institute of Architects' highest national award, The Inn at Middleton Place offers secluded accommodations in 55 rooms. Located adjacent to the Gardens, the Inn supports the mission of the Middleton Place Foundation. Complementing the Foundation's conservation work, the Inn management has developed an ecologically-based program of kayaking, bicycling, hiking, horseback riding and nature studies.

MIDDLETON PLACE FOUNDATION

4300 Ashley River Road, Charleston, South Carolina 29414-7206
(843) 556-6020 or (800) 782-3608

WWW.MIDDLETONPLACE.ORG